ARMENIA: HUMAN RIGHTS

EXECUTIVE SUMMARY

Armenia's constitution provides for a republic with an elected head of state and a unicameral legislature, the National Assembly. The country held a presidential election on February 18, and the OSCE Office for Democratic Institutions and Human Rights (ODIHR) described the election as administered in an overall professional, open, and transparent manner with respect for fundamental freedoms, but marked by shortcomings including an uneven playing field, some serious election day violations, and concerns about the integrity of the electoral process. Authorities maintained effective control over security forces; some members of security forces committed human rights abuses.

The most significant human rights problems during the year were corruption and lack of transparency in government, limitations on the right of citizens to change their government, and the limited independence of the judiciary. Allegations of persistent corruption at all levels of government undermined the rule of law, although the government took limited steps to punish corruption by low- and mid-level officials. Despite candidates' ability to campaign freely, flaws in the conduct of the presidential election included a lack of impartiality by the public administration, the misuse of government resources to support the ruling party, credible allegations of vote buying, continued shortcomings in the implementation of the electoral code, and a complaints and appeals process that failed to provide for effective redress. OSCE/ODIHR also noted a tendency of significantly better final results for the incumbent in the majority of stations with above-average turnout, indicating "possible serious problems with voting and counting" which raised "concerns about the integrity of the electoral process." Courts remained subjected to political pressure from the executive branch, which resulted in some politically motivated prosecutions and sentencing, and the Court of Cassation exercised considerable control over judges' decisions at all levels.

Other abuses reported during the year included suspicious deaths in the military under noncombat conditions, continued hazing and other mistreatment of conscripts by officers and fellow soldiers, and lack of accountability for such actions. Police allegedly continued to employ torture to obtain confessions and reportedly beat citizens during arrest and interrogation. Many prisons were overcrowded, unsanitary, and lacking in medical services for inmates. Authorities continued to arrest and detain criminal suspects without reasonable suspicion and to detain individuals arbitrarily. Trials were often lengthy, and courts failed to enforce laws providing for fair trials. Authorities did not adequately enforce laws against government intrusion on the right to privacy and unlawful searches. Outside of the pre-election period, media coverage during the year lacked diversity of political opinion. While the government released all imprisoned Jehovah's Witnesses, government restrictions affected some minority religious groups, although most registered religious groups reported no significant legal impediments to their activities. Members of religious minorities suffered from societal discrimination. Domestic violence remained a problem but largely went unreported to authorities. Human trafficking was a problem, but authorities made efforts to combat it. Persons with disabilities experienced discrimination in almost all areas of life. Military and prison authorities subjected lesbian, gay, bisexual, and transgender (LGBT) persons to abuse and discrimination; societal discrimination also was a problem. The government limited workers' rights and weakly enforced labor laws.

Although the government took some steps to punish officials in the security forces and elsewhere who committed abuses, some members of the security forces continued to commit human rights abuses with impunity while under the direction of civilian leadership. As of year's end, authorities had not held anyone accountable for the 10 deaths that occurred following postelection clashes in 2008.

Section 1. Respect for the Integrity of the Person, Including Freedom from:

a. Arbitrary or Unlawful Deprivation of Life

There were no reports that the government or its agents committed arbitrary or unlawful killings, but noncombat deaths in the army continued to be a problem. The government reported 10 cases involving fatalities during the first nine months of the year under noncombat conditions. The military prosecutor investigates deaths in the military.

On July 31, the Ministry of Defense reported the death from gunshot wounds of conscript Manuchar Manucharyan. The investigation department of the ministry launched a criminal case on charges of inducing to suicide, despite reports that Manucharyan suffered three gunshot wounds to the head. An expert from the Helsinki Association, Ruben Martirosyan, alleged that the investigation department forced Manucharyan's childhood friend to testify that Manucharyan was in love with her, but she rejected him, providing a motive for suicide. Furthermore, according to Martirosyan, investigators discovered no fingerprints on the weapon they found next to Manucharyan's body. Manucharyan's family denied an earlier claim by the investigation department that Manucharyan belonged to a religious minority. As of November, an investigation was in process.

Human rights observers continued to assert that authorities presented sanitized versions of reported incidents of hazing and death in the military and then focused their follow-up investigations on reinforcing the initial versions. According to observers, the armed forces in most cases declined to punish those responsible. According to the NGO Helsinki Association, investigators, prosecutors, and courts at all levels worked as a system to cover up and conceal the real perpetrators of deaths in the military services. Courts reportedly upheld, and prosecutors defended, indictments based on investigations during which investigators illegally detained and forced suspects and witnesses, through physical and psychological abuse, to provide false testimony. Investigators reportedly destroyed or replaced physical evidence and fingerprints.

In July the military prosecutor announced the creation of a working group, composed of NGO representatives and the ombudsman's office, to look into investigations of military deaths concluded since the beginning of 2011. Human rights NGOs had mixed reactions concerning the initiative, and some, including the ombudsman, declined to join the working group given its limited mandate and unclear terms of reference. On September 10, following a few working meetings, two of the NGOs on the commission resigned after the military prosecutor dismissed the case against the son of a former Syunik governor (see section 1.d.).

During the year the trial continued of those charged with the June 2012 death of military doctor Vahe Avetyan. Security guards and personnel of a restaurant owned by former Republican Party member of the National Assembly Ruben Hayrapetyan attacked and beat Avetyan and four others. Lawyers representing Avetyan's family alleged investigators deliberately conducted a cursory and incomplete investigation and brought unusually lenient charges against the perpetrators. Numerous groups alleged that investigators failed to conduct a thorough investigation into Hayrapetyan's involvement in the crime. Six defendants faced trial on charges of infliction of medium and grave injuries and battery. The charges jointly carry a maximum of 15 years' imprisonment.

Separatists, with Armenia's support, continued to control most of Nagorno-Karabakh and seven other Azerbaijani territories. The final status of Nagorno-Karabakh remained the subject of international mediation by the OSCE Minsk Group, cochaired by Russia, France, and the United States.

On May 20, the National Assembly refused to establish a new ad hoc commission to look into the 2008 postelection unrest. As of year's end, authorities had not held anyone accountable for the deaths of eight civilians and two police officers in the aftermath of the 2008 presidential election.

b. Disappearance

There were no reports of politically motivated disappearances.

c. Torture and Other Cruel, Inhuman, or Degrading Treatment or Punishment

While the law prohibits such practices, reports indicated that members of the security forces continued to employ them regularly. Witnesses reported that police beat citizens while arresting and interrogating them. Human rights NGOs made similar allegations but noted most cases of police mistreatment were unreported due to fear of retaliation. Most abuses reportedly took place in police stations, because they were not subject to public monitoring, rather than prisons and police detention facilities, which were. According to NGOs many individuals that authorities transferred to prisons from police facilities alleged that police tortured, abused, and intimidated them while they were in police custody, mainly to extort confessions.

According to a 2012 EU report, "Implementation of the European Neighborhood Policy in Armenia," released on March 20, the law that criminalizes torture does not conform to the definition of torture in the UN Convention against Torture. For example, the law does not include crimes committed by public officials, but only by individuals acting in a private capacity. Accordingly, the country's courts have never convicted a public official on torture charges.

On March 13, the United Nations Children's Fund (UNICEF) presented findings of a study by a number of domestic and international bodies on the mistreatment and torture of juveniles in the juvenile justice system, from their initial apprehension through the completion of sentences. Interviews with 86 juveniles revealed that the most common forms of mistreatment were beating and physical pressure exerted by the police to extract confessions. Eight of the children attested that they had personally experienced violence, and 51 percent of those surveyed heard of the mistreatment of other children, including beating, sexual violence, cursing, intimidation, and threats. According to the report, the children were reluctant to report mistreatment because they feared retaliation and did not trust the system.

Most victims considered the risks involved in making a complaint--exposing themselves to punishment and retaliation--far outweighed the possibility that the perpetrator would be punished.

On May 3, the Helsinki Committee of Armenia presented findings on the treatment of detained persons in police departments, based on discussions and questionnaires with pretrial detainees held in Nubarashen penitentiary. Those who completed questionnaires said that they had undergone either psychological pressure or physical abuse while at various police departments in Yerevan and the regions. None of the persons surveyed reported the abuse at the time of their transfer from police custody to a penitentiary, because police officers were present at the medical examinations that took place at the time of the transfer. Police reportedly forced many detainees to refuse the services of lawyers. According to human rights observers, police often inflicted blows in a manner not to leave traces. Conversations with judges and law enforcement officials within the same study revealed that investigators viewed confessions obtained through violence as the most effective way of solving crimes.

The annual report of the human rights defender (the ombudsman's office) for 2012, released in March, also stated that police investigative bodies continued to subject individuals to cruel, inhuman, and humiliating treatment in order to obtain confessions.

In August the Public Monitoring Group of Police Detention Facilities (PMG), a coalition of NGOs that inspects police detention cells with permission of the authorities, released its annual report covering 2012. According to PMG findings, every third person kept in such cells experienced inhuman or degrading treatment. The report noted that authorities did not always properly carry out medical examinations of persons transferred to police detention cells and arrested persons did not always receive proper medical care. Authorities conducted medical and physical examinations in a degrading manner in the presence of outside persons, and sometimes an accountant, cleaner, or administrative worker conducted the examinations.

On March 14, the country's police chief appointed Ashot Karapetyan as the new police chief of Yerevan. Shortly after the appointment, Grisha Virabyan, who successfully argued in the European Court of Human Rights (ECHR) that Yerevan police tortured him in 2004, announced that one of his torturers, identified during the ECHR proceedings as A.K., was Karapetyan, who at the time was deputy head of the Ararat regional division of the police. Authorities defended the appointment; as of year's end, no one faced charges for Virabyan's mistreatment. Human rights observers and media criticized the Karapetyan appointment, noting that it reinforced widely held beliefs concerning the lack of accountability for human rights abuses by police.

Karapetyan's name appeared in another case of alleged police abuse. On September 13, media reported that a court of appeals ordered law enforcement bodies to investigate allegations that police tortured Harutyun Sargsyan, a suspect in the April 2012 high-profile killing of Karen Yesayan, the fiance of the daughter of the former mayor of Gyumri. According to Sargsyan's father, Gyumri police, under the leadership of regional police chief Karen Babakekhyan, tortured his son to extort a confession, and the mistreatment continued after his transfer to the Yerevan police detention facility. Sargysyan's father asserted that police beat Sargsyan so badly that his feet did not fit his shoes due to swelling, and he suffered multiple other injuries including a fractured bone above his ear. Although authorities did not record the alleged injuries in the detention facility, Sargsyan repeated these claims of abuse in court. One of the alleged abusers in Yerevan reportedly identified himself to his victim as the head of the General Department of Criminal Investigation, a position held at the time by Ashot Karapetyan. As of November Sargsyan's trial for murder continued.

In July 2012 the UN Human Rights Committee expressed concern about the absence of a genuinely independent mechanism to investigate allegations of torture or other mistreatment in detention facilities as well as about the low number of prosecutions of such cases.

Within the armed forces, substandard living conditions, corruption, and lack of accountability of commanders continued to contribute to mistreatment and noncombat injuries. Although no reliable statistics on the prevalence of military hazing were available, soldiers reported to human rights organizations that abuses continued. Soldiers' families claimed that corrupt officials controlled military units, and human rights monitors and the ombudsman reported the government continued to conscript soldiers with serious health conditions that should have disqualified them from service.

Prison and Detention Center Conditions

Overcrowding, inadequate sanitary conditions and medical care, and corruption remained problems in prisons, and conditions in some cases were harsh and life threatening.

Physical Conditions: The average prison population during the first nine months of the year was 4,742. The capacity of all penal institutions was 4,395 persons.

During the first nine months of the year, the Abovian penitentiary for women and juveniles held an average of 203 women and 24 juveniles (of which one was female). There were no separate facilities for female juvenile convicts, mainly because there rarely were juvenile convicts. When there were such convicts, authorities held them together with adult women. Inmates at the Abovian penitentiary lived in large dormitories, with women housed separately from juvenile boys. According to domestic observers, the group arrangement for women generated conditions that were worse than those at penitentiaries where inmates had separate cells.

According to the PMG's 2012 report, overcrowding in police detention cells and the use of these cells as holding centers for pretrial detainees remained a problem. Outside of Yerevan pretrial detainees outnumbered arrestees in such cells by more than two to one--2,055 of the former compared to 816 of the latter. While the report covered police detention cells, police stations were not included because authorities did not permit the PMG to monitor them.

According to official data, the number of deaths in prisons during the first nine months of the year was 14, with the cause of death listed as illness in 11 cases, suicide in two cases, and one due to injuries resulting from a fall. According to human rights organizations, overcrowding, the poor condition of the buildings, and negligence in providing health care to inmates contributed to the death rate. Prisons had connections to local potable water supplies but experienced occasional service disruptions.

In December the Helsinki Committee of Armenia published research on prison conditions based on interviews with 33 former male convicts who served their sentences in various penitentiaries. According to the report, rampant corruption affected every aspect of prison life. The penitentiary system, while formally operating under the Ministry of Justice, remained outside the ministry's control, with the president directly appointing the chief of the penitentiary system. The report concluded that authorities at all levels lacked the political will to improve the system significantly.

Prison administrators and guards were underpaid and reportedly used a clandestine system to extract bribes from prisoners for basic services and privileges. For example, convicts paid bribes to obtain a better cell, take showers, visit other cells, avoid cell inspections, obtain medicine and narcotics, have a television set, keep a mobile phone, or be transferred to the prison hospital. According to various accounts, a transfer to the prison hospital, which had somewhat better conditions, required a bribe of $500 to $1,000. Former convicts faced harassment following their release, with police pressuring and subjecting them to violence following every theft in their areas.

The Helsinki Committee's research also discussed the harsh living conditions in penitentiaries. In some cases cells with 10 or 12 beds held 23 or 24 convicts, and some prisoners slept on floors or in chairs. Of the 33 former prisoners interviewed, 20 developed health complications during their incarceration. Prison food was inedible, and inmates ate food brought by relatives. Inmates bought or received hygiene products from outside the prison. Medical services were poor, and prisoners received medical attention only when in grave condition.

On March 18, Arthur Ayvazyan, a convict serving a term at Nubarashen Penitentiary, attempted to commit suicide by cutting his veins after abuse by penitentiary staff. After the incident prison staff refused to let medical personnel into his cell to provide assistance, and one of his cellmates had to cut his own veins to ensure medical personnel got to Ayvazyan. The prosecutor's office rejected a motion by Ayvazyan's lawyer to open a criminal case for inducing suicide.

In October 2012 the Council of Europe's Committee for the Prevention of Torture (CPT) released a report describing its 2011 follow-up visit to Kentron and Nubarashen prisons. The CPT found authorities had failed to implement most of the recommendations concerning prisoners serving life sentences that it made following its 2010 visit.

Administration: There were no reports that authorities employed measures such as alternative sentencing for nonviolent offenders, although they did allow early release and release on parole. Human rights activists and attorneys continued to voice concern over the performance of the commissions on early release and release on parole. The Chamber of Advocates, the country's bar association, protested the absence of criteria to guide the commissions' decisions and withdrew its representatives from the commissions in January 2012. The absence of an appeal mechanism and the overrepresentation of law enforcement representatives on the commissions also remained obstacles to due process. According to the Helsinki Committee report, former inmates attested that prisoners needed to pay substantial bribes in order to secure early release.

There were no reports of efforts to improve prison recordkeeping.

The Civil Society Monitoring Board for penitentiaries, consisting of NGO representatives, continued reporting to the Ministry of Justice on the deteriorating health of convicts who the board claimed remained in prison although they qualified for early release on medical grounds. The interagency medical commission in charge of considering the early release of prisoners on health grounds was generally very slow to act and did not have established procedures for its activities.

Prisons did not have ombudsmen.

Human rights organizations and the human rights defender's office continued to raise concerns that convicts and detainees did not always have reasonable access to visitors, since overcrowded conditions and lack of suitable space deprived them of even their minimal visitation entitlement. Prisoners could engage in religious observance.

Authorities did not always permit prisoners and detainees to submit uncensored appeals to authorities concerning credible allegations of inhuman conditions, although the prevalence of such censorship was unknown. By law censorship of the communications of pretrial detainees requires a court order. According to human rights organizations, prison administrators censored the letters of detainees in numerous cases without judicial oversight. According to human rights NGOs, authorities did not investigate credible allegations of inhuman conditions. According to the report of the Helsinki Committee of Armenia on prison conditions, prisoners could send uncensored letters if they paid a bribe.

Independent Monitoring: The government generally permitted domestic and international human rights groups, including the CPT, to monitor prison and detention center conditions. They could speak to prisoners privately. The government permitted the International Committee of the Red Cross to visit both prisons and pretrial detention centers.

d. Arbitrary Arrest or Detention

The law prohibits arbitrary arrest and detention. Although authorities generally complied with the legal requirement of judicial review, judges were often reluctant to challenge prosecutors' requests to detain individuals or to review police conduct during arrests.

Role of the Police and Security Apparatus

The national police force is responsible for internal security, while the National Security Service is responsible for national security, intelligence activities, and border control. The president appoints the heads of both organizations, and they report directly to him.

Police and the National Security Service continued to lack sufficient training, resources, and established procedures to prevent abuse. Impunity was a problem; there was no dedicated independent mechanism for investigating police abuse. In July 2012 the UN Human Rights Committee noted its concern about the lack of accountability of law enforcement officers in cases of excessive use of force and the lack of an independent mechanism for investigating police abuse.

Citizens may sue police, but this avenue is limited. Prior to trial defendants have the legal right to file complaints alleging that law enforcement personnel abused them in the course of an investigation but must obtain permission from police or the prosecutor's office in order to undergo the forensic medical examination necessary to substantiate an accusation of physical abuse legally. Human rights organizations continued to report that authorities rarely granted such permission or delayed it until physical signs of abuse were no longer visible. NGOs reported that judges routinely ignored defendants' claims that authorities coerced their testimony through physical abuse.

Law enforcement corruption and impunity continued to be problems.

On March 5, the Europe in Law Association and Transparency International issued a joint statement condemning the Special Investigative Service (SIS) for its treatment of presidential election international observer Narine Esmaeili. On February 18, during presidential election monitoring, Esmaeili witnessed election fraud and was assaulted at a precinct in Artashat. Based on her testimony, the Constitutional Court invalidated the results of the election in that precinct. According to NGO and media reports, however, throughout the investigation into the assault and electoral fraud, SIS investigator Gorik Hovakimyan and SIS chief Andranik Mirzoyan demonstrated aggressive behavior toward Esmaeili and her lawyer. Despite the Constitutional Court's decision, on July 26, the court acquitted the only suspect charged in the case, Sergey Muradyan, the son of the Artashat mayor, after the prosecutor dropped all charges against him. On May 2, the president dismissed Mirzoyan from his position reportedly for illicit acts in connection with an unrelated criminal case and failure to complete objectives set for him.

Selective application of the law and impunity for powerful officials were problems. In multiple instances throughout the year, law enforcement bodies refused to prosecute high profile cases involving individuals linked to the government, or the courts gave lenient sentences in such cases.

On June 2, an exchange of gunfire near the house of Syunik governor Surik Khachatryan killed Avetik Budaghyan and seriously injured his brother, military commander Artak Budaghyan, and Khachatryan's bodyguard, Nikolay Abrahamyan. Soon afterwards police arrested Khachatryan's son Tigran Khachatryan and one of Khachatryan's bodyguards, Zarzand Nikoghosyan, on charges of murder. Police confiscated large quantities of weapons from the governor's house. Surik Khachatryan, who resigned following the arrest, claimed that he was asleep during the shooting. On June 5, before the investigation was complete, the then military prosecutor Gevorg Kostanyan publicly stated that the governor was not at the site of the incident and suggested that the incident resulted from an armed attack on the governor's house. On September 7, the Ministry of Defense announced that it was dropping all charges against Tigran Khachatryan and Zarzand Nikoghosyan, as their actions constituted self defense. According to Budaghyan's lawyer, authorities based their decision solely on the testimony of the suspects and Khachatryan's family. Artak Budaghyan faced charges of threat to murder, to inflict heavy damage to one's health, or to destroy property. According to Budaghyan's lawyer, the investigators directed the inquiry to clear the Khachatryan family of any responsibility.

Arrest Procedures and Treatment of Detainees

Authorities on occasion detained and arrested criminal suspects without arrest warrants and without reasonable suspicion. By law an investigative body must either formally arrest or release an individual within three hours of taking him or her into custody. Within 72 hours the investigative body must release the arrested person or bring charges and obtain a detention warrant from a judge. Judges rarely denied police requests for detention warrants. Police routinely summoned individuals and held them longer than three hours without formally arresting them under the pretext that they were material witnesses rather than suspects. Domestic observers contended police avoided labeling summoned persons as suspects to avoid the legal requirement to grant them the rights of suspects.

The law requires police to inform detainees of their right to remain silent, to make a telephone call, and to representation by an attorney from the moment of arrest. The law entitles detainees to public defenders if they are indigent. Police often questioned and pressured detainees to confess to crimes prior to indicting them and in the absence of legal counsel. According to the PMG, few detainees knew about their right to legal representation. The practice of detaining individuals as "material witnesses" before designating them as suspects allowed authorities to question them without the benefit of a defense attorney.

In July 2012 the UN Human Rights Committee criticized the frequent use of pretrial detention and stated that authorities did not fully inform detainees of their rights and frequently deprived them of timely access to a lawyer and a medical doctor. The committee noted that authorities did not promptly bring detainees before a judge.

According to the PMG's 2012 report, police held one-third of individuals they detained for four to 52 hours before formally arresting them. According to the report, only 10.4 percent of those held in police detention cells, including persons under pretrial detention, used the services of an attorney.

The law provides a bail system, but courts generally denied requests for bail and ordered that defendants remain in pretrial detention. In some cases authorities released defendants on their own recognizance pending trial, with the requirement that they surrender their passports and sign statements promising not to leave the country or, in some cases, city limits.

Arbitrary Arrest: The UN Human Rights Council's (UNHRC) Working Group on Arbitrary Detention noted in a 2011 report that police, National Security Service personnel, and border guards often detained or arrested individuals without an arrest warrant. Arrests were often not a consequence of a police investigation; rather, authorities held individuals to initiate an investigation, often in the hope that the suspect would confess, thus making further investigation unnecessary.

Pretrial Detention: Lengthy pretrial or preventive detention remained a chronic problem. According to official information, during the first nine months of the year an average of 6.7 percent of the prison population consisted of pretrial detainees and an additional 9.6 percent were detainees whose trials were in progress.

Although the law requires detention decisions to be reasonable and detention to be used as a measure of last resort, attorneys and court observers complained that detention was often approved routinely by courts with little consideration as to whether less restrictive alternatives might suffice. The overuse of detention applied also to juvenile offenders. There is no separate system of justice for juvenile offenders.

Although the law requires a well-reasoned justification for extending pretrial custody every two months, judges routinely granted extensions on unclear grounds. Authorities generally respected the provision limiting total pretrial detention to 12 months. The law does not establish time limits on the detention of defendants once prosecutors forward their cases to court. According to the UNHRC's 2011 report, prosecutors regularly requested and received trial postponements from judges, arguing that they required more time to prepare for trial, that is, to prolong investigations. Prosecutors tended to blame defense lawyers and their requests for more time to prepare a defense for trial postponements.

Amnesty: On October 3, the National Assembly adopted a general amnesty proposed by the president, resulting in the release of 558 convicts from prisons as of October 18.

e. Denial of Fair Public Trial

The law provides for an independent judiciary. In practice courts remained subject to political pressure from the executive branch as well as the expectation that judges would find the accused guilty in almost every case. The UNHRC reported in 2011 that the government's fight against corruption also had negative implications for the independence of judges, who appeared to be ordering harsh penalties due to fear that any sign of leniency would arouse suspicion they had taken bribes.

The judiciary was not independent, and judges lacked effective legal remedies if executive, legislative, or more senior judicial authorities decided to punish them. The vulnerability of judges to dismissal, combined with the absence of any effective remedy for such treatment and uncertainty about receiving a pension, had a strong chilling effect on the judiciary and its independence.

The Council of Justice, headed by the chair of the Cassation Court, appoints and dismisses judges and may charge a judge with miscarriage of justice, even for a ruling that neither party appealed to a higher court or in which the appellate courts found no errors. The decisions of the council are not subject to review. There were reports that the Cassation Court dictated the outcome of all significant cases to lower court judges. According to a January statement by the ombudsman, judges could ignore the law, decisions of the Constitutional Courts, and international legal norms, but not the internal, often illegal, directives of the Cassation Court. According to observers the Cassation Court's control over judicial decisions remained an overarching problem affecting judicial independence.

There was no progress during the year in the efforts of former judge Surik Ghazaryan to have his pension reinstated. In 2011, according to credible sources, Chief Justice Arman Mkrtumyan, the head of the Cassation Court, forced Ghazaryan to resign and lose his pension in retaliation for not consulting with the Cassation Court prior to his 2010 ruling in a high-profile case involving the interests of Yukos Oil Company and Rosneft (Russia's state-owned oil company). The ruling favored Yukos Oil Company.

During the year the criminal proceedings remained pending against Armen Mikayelyan, a former director of Yukos CIS Ltd. (the Armenian subsidiary of Yukos Oil Company), on charges of abuse of authority by employees of commercial or other organizations. According to credible sources, the government charged Mikayelyan at the direct request of the Russian firm Rosneft to exert pressure on Mikayelyan to cooperate with Rosneft's efforts to take over the assets of Yukos CIS Ltd.

Authorities generally complied with court orders.

Trials usually met many of the procedural standards for fairness. They were often unfair in substance, however, because many judges felt compelled to work with prosecutors to achieve convictions. Judges were reluctant to challenge police experts or hold the prosecution accountable for meeting an appropriately high standard of guilt, thereby hampering a defendant's ability to mount a credible defense.

Trial Procedures

The law provides for the presumption of innocence, but authorities did not respect this right. The law requires that most trials be public but permits exceptions, including in the interest of "morals," national security, and for the "protection of the private lives of the participants." Juries are not used; a single judge issues verdicts in trial courts (except for crimes punishable by life imprisonment), and panels of judges preside in the higher courts. Defendants have the right to counsel of their own choosing, and the law requires the government to provide them with a public defender upon request. A shortage of defense lawyers frequently led to denial of this right outside of Yerevan, although in 2012 the number of public defenders grew from 32 to 52.

By law defendants may confront witnesses, present evidence, and examine the government's case in advance of a trial, but defendants and their attorneys had very little ability to challenge government witnesses. This circumstance was particularly prejudicial to defendants in challenging the evidence gathered by police officers, whom the law prohibits from testifying in their official capacities unless they are a witness or a victim in a case. Courts routinely accepted into evidence official police reports describing the evidence found at a crime scene or the confession of a defendant, without any in-court testimony from police officers. Defense lawyers had almost no ability to challenge the findings of these official reports, which courts generally regarded as unimpeachable. Judges controlled witness lists, which designated the witnesses deemed to have evidence relevant to a criminal case. Defense attorneys complained that at times judges would not allow them to call or obtain the attendance at trial of witnesses whom they believed to have evidence helpful to their client's defense. Defendants, prosecutors, and the injured party have the right of appeal and often exercised it.

On June 10, approximately 200 lawyers went on a two-day strike to protest what they characterized as arbitrary decision making by the Cassation Court. The lawyers criticized the court's refusal, without substantive explanation, to consider the vast majority of their criminal and civil appeals.

The vast majority of criminal cases sent to trial resulted in conviction. Although many weak cases resulted in convictions, the practice by police investigators of declining to forward weak cases to the courts may also have played a role in the high conviction rate. The acquittal rate during the first nine months of the year was 1.6 percent.

Political Prisoners and Detainees

During the year, local human rights observers claimed that the unusual severity of the sentences given to four opposition Armenian National Congress youth activists involved in a 2011 altercation with police was politically motivated. By year's end, judicial authorities had amnestied Artak Karapetyan and Tigran Arakelyan, and given Davit Kiramijyan and Sargis Gevorgyan two years of suspended sentences with one year of probation.

Civil Judicial Procedures and Remedies

Although citizens had access to courts to bring lawsuits seeking damages for, or cessation of, human rights violations, the courts were widely perceived as corrupt. Citizens also had access to the Office of the Human Rights Defender (ombudsman), as well as the possibility of challenging the constitutionality of legislation in the Constitutional Court. The Constitutional Court exercised its power to determine the constitutionality of statutes in dozens of cases during the year, but lower courts enforced its decisions unevenly, because they are subordinate to the Cassation Court rather than the Constitutional Court.

Regional Human Rights Court Decisions: Citizens who exhaust domestic legal remedies can appeal cases involving alleged government violations of the European Convention on Human Rights to the ECHR. Dozens of appeals were pending before the court at year's end. As of November 18, the ECHR issued judgments in two cases involving the country and found violations of the convention by the state in one case.

The government generally complied with the ECHR awards of monetary compensation. The government did not reopen cases on which the ECHR had ruled, and courts often did not follow the applicable ECHR precedent.

f. Arbitrary Interference with Privacy, Family, Home, or Correspondence

The constitution prohibits unauthorized searches and provides for the rights to privacy and confidentiality of communications. There were unconfirmed reports that law enforcement bodies tapped the telephone communications and e-mail correspondence of individuals, including human rights activists and members of the political opposition, whom the government wanted to keep under scrutiny.

Law enforcement bodies may not legally wiretap a telephone, intercept correspondence, or conduct searches without obtaining the permission of a judge. Law enforcement bodies generally adhered to legal procedures, but human rights observers indicated there were instances when police conducted searches at homes without warrants under the pretext of looking for wanted persons. According to attorneys judges often authorized wiretaps, the interception of correspondence, and searches without receiving the compelling evidence of criminal activity required by law, rendering legal procedures largely a formality.

Section 2. Respect for Civil Liberties, Including:

a. Freedom of Speech and Press

The government did not always uphold these rights. Media, including print, online, and broadcast, was controlled by, or generally expressed views sympathetic to, the government. There were multiple incidents of violence toward journalists in connection with the February 18 presidential election, the May 5 municipal elections, and citizens' protests throughout the year.

Freedom of Speech: On June 10, the progovernment Shant TV station fired news anchor Armen Dulyan after he posted material on social media that drew parallels between the media situation in Russia and Armenia and suggested that authorities in both countries controlled most television stations. In dismissing Dulyan Shant TV stated that further cooperation with him was unacceptable, given the attitude he had displayed toward the company. Many journalists criticized the dismissal, noting that the incident appeared to substantiate the accusation that Shant TV was under government control and intolerant of free speech and thought.

Press Freedoms: Except for the four-week official campaign periods preceding the February presidential and May municipal elections, when broadcast media provided diverse and objective media coverage, traditional media for the most part continued to lack diversity of political opinion and objective reporting.

Newspaper circulation remained limited. Private persons or groups owned most newspapers, with the exception of the government-sponsored *Hayastani Hanrapetutyun* and its Russian-language edition, *Respublika Armenii.* Most publications tended to reflect the political leanings of their proprietors and financial backers, who were often close to the government. The political factions and business interests that sponsored these publications showed little interest in developing fair and balanced nationwide coverage. Only a handful of newspapers operated as efficient and self-sustaining enterprises.

Broadcast media, particularly national television, remained the primary source of news and information for the majority of the population. The audience for the country's 20 radio stations, three of which were public and one broadcasting from abroad, remained limited. Private interests owned all but three of the 97 television stations in operation during the year; most were small and based in outlying regions. Four stations rebroadcast content from abroad. Politicians in the ruling party or politically connected executives owned most stations, and the stations presented one-sided views of events. Regional television channels provided some alternative viewpoints, often through externally produced content.

During the year the government did not carry out its promise to release the audit of the country's television and radio frequencies that provided the technical basis for limiting the number of digital broadcasting licenses it will permit after the country switches from analog to digital transmission, planned for 2015. On June 19, the National Assembly adopted amendments to the law on television and radio that delayed by six months the suspension of analog broadcasting initially scheduled for January 1, 2015.

Online media outlets were the primary alternative source of information, and unlike broadcast media, provided diverse political opinions. The government did not generally control their content; nonetheless, their broadcasts often reflected the political influence of sponsors or advertisers. There were credible reports of continuing consolidation of both online and broadcast media outlets by a few government-affiliated individuals.

Violence and Harassment: There were several incidents of violence against reporters covering the February 18 presidential and May 5 municipal elections and the ongoing citizens' protests throughout the year.

On April 23, a group of young men in Yerevan's Nor Nork District attacked Hakob Karapetyan, a reporter with the opposition-leaning website iLur.am, as he was trying to film a campaign rally of the ruling Republican Party prior to city council elections. According to press reports, the attackers seized Karapetyan's camera and erased its contents. Karapetyan suffered bodily injury. Republican Party city council representative Ashot Papyan led the attackers. A few days later, police, who opened an investigation into the incident as well as an internal inquiry into reported police inaction during it, dismissed Gagik Amirjanyan, the deputy chief of Nor Nork's police department, and reprimanded two lower-ranking officials. On July 5, police announced that, by mutual agreement of the parties, they were dropping criminal charges against the attackers for hindering a journalist's professional activities.

On May 20, leading media organizations issued a statement criticizing law enforcement bodies that reportedly used violence to obstruct the efforts of reporters and camera crews from a number of media outlets to cover protests of the family of a soldier allegedly killed by a fellow conscript. On May 21, in an interview with the Public Radio of Armenia, the president's spokesperson criticized the treatment of the journalists, expressing confidence that the relevant organizations would undertake all necessary means to "disclose the circumstances of the case." According to official information, authorities launched a criminal case over the seizure of one reporter's camera but later dropped the case since the perpetrator was unknown.

On July 24, the National Security Service dropped charges of money laundering and misappropriation of funds against Vardan Oskanian, former head of the Civilitas Foundation and former foreign minister. Authorities originally charged Oskanian in May 2012, immediately after his party, Prosperous Armenia, announced its decision not to join the ruling coalition. The Civilitas Foundation operated one of the largest independent online media outlets, CivilNet. Many observers described the investigation and its timing as politically motivated.

Censorship and Content Restrictions: Media outlets, particularly broadcasters, feared reprisals for reporting critical of the government. Such reprisals could include lawsuits, the threat of losing a broadcast license, selective tax investigation, or loss of revenue when advertisers learned an outlet was in disfavor with the government. Fear of retribution led to a high degree of media self-censorship.

Libel Laws/National Security: A 2011 recommendation by the Constitutional Court that courts avoid levying disproportionately heavy fines in libel and defamation cases resulted in smaller damages awarded to those who sued media outlets.

Internet Freedom

There were no government restrictions on access to the internet or credible reports that the government monitored e-mail or internet chat rooms without appropriate legal authority. Individuals and groups could generally engage in the expression of views via the internet, including by e-mail. During the year certain websites, including independent Hetq, Gala TV, the Iditord citizen-run election monitoring website, and those of other NGOs, reported cyber attacks.

According to the International Telecommunication Union, 39 percent of the population used the internet in 2012.

Academic Freedom and Cultural Events

There were some reports of government restrictions on academic freedom and cultural events.

On February 25, the media reported that the Yerevan State College of Informatics dismissed Hovhannes Ghazaryan for his participation in student strikes. On March 15, the media reported that Yerevan State University did not extend its contract with Professor Ararat Mirzoyan, allegedly because of negative statements he made about the behavior of the rector's assistant, Gevorg Melkonyan, during a student strike on February 27.

Society generally viewed most prominent state universities as highly politicized and affiliated with the ruling Republican Party. For example, the chairman of the board of Yerevan State University was President Serzh Sargsyan, and the rector of the University, Aram Simonyan, was a member of the Republican Party board.

b. Freedom of Peaceful Assembly and Association

Freedom of Assembly

The constitution and the law provide for freedom of assembly; while the government frequently respected this right, authorities reportedly took measures to impede participation at some rallies, and there were reported incidents of excessive force used against demonstrators.

There were isolated reports that local authorities blocked opposition political rallies or gave preferential treatment to progovernment events during the campaign prior to the February 18 elections. There were reports that local authorities blocked civil servants from attending opposition rallies, and there were widespread reports that government officials compelled public servants and students to attend progovernment rallies. There were also allegations that authorities restricted travel along roads leading to the sites of opposition rallies.

The police and local authorities generally respected the rights of individuals to organize rallies, including after the election, when opposition parties organized a series of unauthorized rallies in Yerevan and elsewhere in the country. Throughout the year police videotaped participants attending political rallies, both in the regions and in Yerevan. According to local observers, this deliberately visible surveillance had a chilling effect on citizens' willingness to participate in political rallies and to exercise their right of freedom of expression. There were also reports that administrators of a state-run university locked students inside a university building to prevent them from attending a rally protesting the conduct of the presidential election.

There were some complaints that police used excessive force against protesters in isolated incidents. Some observers complained that police used excessive force on April 9 to prevent protesters from approaching the presidential palace during an inaugural day event attended by international dignitaries. Footage from the event showed police officers kneeing a member of the board of the opposition Heritage Party, Armen Martirosyan, in the face. According to unofficial reports, authorities removed two police officers involved in the incident from duty. There were similar complaints about the use of excessive force against demonstrators during civic protests in August and in the fall.

On December 2, the day of the visit to the country by the Russian president, law enforcement bodies disrupted a group of 500 to 1,000 persons who intended to march in protest against the decision of the authorities to join the Russian-led Eurasian Customs Union. During the day the police detained 110 persons, including demonstrators, journalists covering the march, activists posting banners throughout the town, and some onlookers who happened to be at the vicinity of demonstrations or near the presidential palace. The police released all of those detained after holding them for several hours and charging them with administrative violations. The ombudsman released a statement on December 3, condemning the police actions.

On July 15, administrative court judge Ruzanna Hakobyan ruled that police violated the rights of Levon Barseghyan, president of the Asparez Journalists Club, when they detained him as he was participating in a small protest march in 2011 against foreign participation in a military parade marking 20 years of national independence. In an unprecedented decision, Judge Hakobyan noted that the police actions violated Barseghyan's rights to freedom of expression, freedom of speech, freedom of association, freedom of assembly, freedom of movement, and his right to personal freedom and security. The police did not appeal the decision.

c. Freedom of Religion

See the Department of State's *International Religious Freedom Report* at www.state.gov/j/drl/irf/rpt/.

d. Freedom of Movement, Internally Displaced Persons, Protection of Refugees, and Stateless Persons

The law provides for freedom of movement within the country, foreign travel, emigration, and repatriation. There were some reports of limited restrictions connected with travel to political rallies. Authorities cooperated with the Office of the UN High Commissioner for Refugees and other humanitarian organizations in providing protection and assistance to refugees, returning refugees and asylum seekers, stateless persons, and other persons of concern.

In-country Movement: During the year there were reports authorities restricted freedom of movement by preventing citizens residing outside Yerevan from traveling to attend opposition rallies in the capital. There were also isolated reports that local authorities restricted travel within districts to prevent attendance at political rallies.

Foreign Travel: Citizens must obtain exit visas to leave the country on a temporary or permanent basis. Citizens could routinely purchase exit visas for temporary travel out of the country within one day of application for approximately 1,000 drams ($2.44) for each year of validity.

Internally Displaced Persons (IDPs)

During the country's war with Azerbaijan over Nagorno-Karabakh, authorities evacuated approximately 65,000 households from the border region, but most IDPs later returned to their homes or settled elsewhere. During a visit to the country in 2010, a UN representative specializing in the human rights of IDPs cited a lack of adequate housing and limited economic opportunities as remaining obstacles faced by some of the country's IDPs and former refugees.

Protection of Refugees

Access to Asylum: The law provides for granting asylum or refugee status, and the government has established a system for providing protection to refugees. The law has a number of shortcomings, and human rights observers contended that asylum procedures required improvement in order to meet international standards. Information about access to the territory for potential asylum-seekers who are not of Armenian origin was rather limited.

The State Migration Service operates a reception center for asylum seekers and is responsible for registering them and adjudicating their asylum applications. The service designed the center for a maximum of 45 persons, but it held more than that number during the year. Those whom the center could not accommodate did not receive food packages from the authorities.

As of mid-year reports indicated that an estimated 10,000 persons from Syria, almost all ethnic Armenians, had arrived in the country since the beginning of the Syrian civil war. As of mid-year of the 718 ethnic Armenians from Syria who applied to the State Migration Service for asylum, 471 had received refugee status and 103 awaited decisions. Authorities closed the cases of 144 individuals for various reasons, including withdrawal of their applications and return to their home country. The vast majority of the remaining ethnic Armenians from Syria received Armenian citizenship or long-term residency permits, although it was unclear how many Syrian-Armenians remained in the country.

Refugee Abuse: In July 2012 the UN Human Rights Committee expressed concern that the government prosecuted some asylum seekers for illegal entry, despite identifying themselves as persons seeking asylum. Authorities did not generally release asylum seekers serving sentences for illegal entry into the country after registering their asylum applications but required them to serve the remainder of their sentences.

Routine rejection of the applications of asylum seekers who were not of ethnic Armenian origin, often on grounds of national security, continued to be the norm.

Access to Basic Services: Authorities often had difficulty integrating refugees into society once the refugees obtained permanent-resident status. Housing allocated to refugees from the 1991-94 conflict over Nagorno-Karabakh was often inadequate in supply and in poor condition. Refugees faced many of the same social and economic hardships that confronted the general population, further exacerbated by language barriers. Syrian-Armenians speak a different dialect of Armenian and speak Arabic rather than Russian as a second language. Relatively easy access to Armenian citizenship did not solve all integration problems, including the social and economic effect of displacement on the refugee populations. The relatively small number of refugees who were not of Armenian origin had even more limited prospects for local integration.

Stateless Persons

According to the UNHCR, as of the end of 2012, there were 35 stateless persons with residency permits in the country. Additionally, 1,716 refugees from Azerbaijan were also stateless. There continued to be individual cases of statelessness when individuals renounced Armenian citizenship without possessing another foreign nationality. Applicants applying for naturalization did not have the right to appeal rejections. There was no clear procedure for the determination of statelessness and no national legislation on the rights of stateless persons.

Section 3. Respect for Political Rights: The Right of Citizens to Change Their Government

Although the constitution and law provide citizens with the right to change their government peacefully, the government continued to interfere with that right during elections.

Elections and Political Participation

Recent Elections: A presidential election took place on February 18. Reports of voters being bribed, large-scale abuse of administrative resources to favor incumbents, concerns about impostors voting in place of absentee voters, and the presence of unauthorized organized groups at many precincts undermined the integrity of the election process and discredited the institution of elections in the public eye.

The OSCE's ODIHR observed the presidential election. In its final election observation report, released on May 8, ODIHR noted that the election "was generally well-administered and was characterized by a respect for fundamental freedoms" but marked by shortcomings including a lack of impartiality by the public administration, misuse of administrative resources, and cases of pressure on voters. Election day was marked by undue interference in the process, mainly by proxies representing the incumbent, and some serious violations were observed. ODIHR also noted that, according to the final election results, the incumbent received more than 50 percent in 40 of 249 stations where turnout was below 50 percent, while Raffi Hovannisyan received more than 50 percent in 155 of these 249 stations. In precincts with turnout of 70 percent or more, the incumbent's share of votes also was 70 percent or more. ODIHR found this close correlation between high voter turnout and higher results for the incumbent indicated "possible serious problems with voting and counting" that raised "concerns about the integrity of the electoral process." National authorities had not addressed any of ODIHR's recommendations by year's end.

Observers were also critical of the complaints and appeals process. In its final election observation report, ODIHR stated, "the right to file election-related complaints is unduly restricted…(and the) adjudication of complaints by the Central Election Commission revealed a persistent application of an overly formalistic approach, whereby it found all complaints to be either inadmissible or without merit. The adjudication of electoral disputes failed to provide for effective redress and to ensure legal integrity." Election commissions and the Constitutional Court rejected most complaints filed after the election as either unsubstantiated or not involving enough votes to influence the outcome.

In addition to procedural problems, ODIHR noted that that there was a low level of public trust in the electoral process. On March 14, the Constitutional Court, which rejected the election complaints filed by presidential candidates Raffi Hovhannisian and Andreas Ghukasyan, also noted the low level of public trust in the electoral process.

The ODHIR report considered the country's 10-year citizenship and residency requirements for candidates to be excessive. There were also concerns that the authorities used administrative resources and selective prosecution or the threat of it to discourage credible candidates from challenging incumbents.

Observers noted that media coverage of the campaign was fair overall, but stressed the lack of debates "depriving voters of the opportunity to see meaningful dialogue that could address contestants' platforms or the incumbents' performance in office." The OSCE/ODIHR reported that there appeared to be equal access to media for parties during the official campaign period, but that the main broadcast media's coverage of post-election events tended to limit views critical of the conduct of the election.

Political Parties: There were no reports of undue legal restrictions on the registration or activity of political parties. Nevertheless, there were continued complaints that the government used its administrative and legal resources to discourage financial contributions to opposition parties, thereby limiting their activities. The inability of opposition parties to raise money either through state funding or through private donations due to government pressure continued to marginalize the opposition parties even further.

There were complaints that well-connected business owners funneled a portion of their profits to parties in the ruling coalition in return for unfair advantage in the form of light or no taxation. Additionally, there were allegations that the government discriminated against members of opposition political parties in hiring decisions.

Participation of Women and Minorities: In July 2012 the UN Human Rights Committee noted its continued concern about the low level of participation by women in political life and in decision-making posts in the public sector. At year's end there were 14 women in the 131-seat National Assembly, two in the cabinet, and no female governors. Only 10 of the 65 elected Yerevan City Council members were women, and no women headed any of Yerevan's 12 administrative districts.

Section 4. Corruption and Lack of Transparency in Government

The law provides criminal penalties for corruption by officials, but the government did not implement the law effectively, and many officials engaged in corrupt practices with impunity. Civic groups working to address corruption stated that authorities continued to ignore media and other reports implicating government officials in corrupt practices, which served to undermine public trust.

In July 2012 the UN Human Rights Committee expressed its concern about allegations that corruption persisted in all branches of the government. The committee stated that the lack of convincing results in the fight against high-level corruption undermined public trust in the administration of justice. Corruption had a significant effect on economic growth. The World Economic Forum's "Global Competitiveness Report for 2013-14" listed corruption as the most problematic factor for doing business in the country.

Corruption: At year's end there was no investigation into the corruption case involving Vardan Ayvazyan, member of the National Assembly and chair of its Standing Committee on Economic Affairs, despite a 2012 foreign court verdict that fined him $37.5 million for demanding a bribe from the Global Gold Mining Company when he was minister of the environment.

In May *Hetq* published a series of articles describing an alleged case of embezzlement and fraud involving domestic commercial banks transferring loans to offshore companies. The articles elicited widespread comment. In one instance a company registered in Cyprus was allegedly a loan recipient. *Hetq* reported that Prime Minister Tigran Sargsyan; the archbishop of the Armenian Apostolic Church, Navasard Kchoyan; and businessperson Ashot Sukiassian jointly owned that company. Sargsyan and Kchoyan denied their participation. In July the prosecutor general officially requested his counterpart in Cyprus to assist in investigating the criminal case he launched into the affair.

In April the NGO Freedom of Information Center of Armenia published information on grants the presidency made to certain NGOs from 2010-12. The presidency awarded 31 NGOs grants totaling 500 million drams ($1.2 million). Media reported that the recipient NGOs existed on paper only, registered shortly before receiving the grants, and were largely founded by the same small group of persons. The Ministry of Justice listed Levon Martirosyan, a member of National Assembly from the Republican Party, as one of the founders of one of the NGOs. Martirosyan worked as an assistant to the president from 2008-12 before election to the National Assembly and was the founder of the United Liberal National Party. Authorities did not open an investigation into the matter during the year. Most other founders of the other 30 NGOs were connected either to Martirosyan or to the United Liberal National Party.

Throughout the year press reports continued about alleged embezzlement and fraud at the Nairit rubber factory. The case involved $180 million in loans that subsequently disappeared through transfers to offshore companies. The media alleged that Minister of Energy Armen Movsisyan was ex officio responsible for overseeing the execution of the loans, and a number of other high-ranking officials reportedly participated in the embezzlement. The Office of the Prosecutor General opened an inquiry and transferred the case to the police unit that fights organized crime, which subsequently closed the case after allegedly finding that no crime had been committed. The government has not provided an explanation for the disappearance of the funds.

Although the constitution and laws prohibit individuals engaged in entrepreneurial activity from holding public office, executives continued to occupy seats in the National Assembly, and various government officials reportedly continued to use their offices to promote their private business interests.

In August *Hetq* published an article alleging that officials in charge of regulation of civil aviation and others linked to them held business interests in the aviation sector through ownership of various airline companies. For example, the deputy head of the General Department of Civil Aviation (GDCA), Aram Marutyan, was the co-owner of Atlantis European Airways. The GDCA had authority to approve new airlines' entry into the market and was heavily involved in the government's civil aviation policy decisions. Reports indicated that Atlantis European Airways received, at no cost, a "soft block" of seats on Austrian Airlines flights between Vienna and Yerevan and on CSA Czech Airlines flights between Prague and Yerevan. The government took no action to investigate or prosecute the GDCA's apparent conflicts of interest.

Police were responsible for investigating corruption, and the prosecutor general was responsible for prosecuting it. According to widespread reports, neither agency operated effectively or independently, and neither was sufficiently resourced.

Whistleblower Protection: There is no special law that protects public or private employees who make internal disclosures or lawful public disclosures of evidence of illegality, such as the solicitation of bribes or other corrupt acts, gross waste or fraud, gross mismanagement, abuse of power, or substantial and specific dangers to public health and safety.

Financial Disclosure: The law requires high-ranking public officials and their families to file annual asset declarations. Pursuant to the law, the Ethics Commission for High-Ranking Officials collects and monitors the declarations, but it has no authority to verify their accuracy or sanction officials for false declarations. There are no criminal penalties for noncompliance or filing false declarations.

Public Access to Information: While the law provides for public access to government information, some government bodies and officials were reluctant to grant it. As of year's end, the government had not adopted the regulations on the collection and provision of information that were required by, and supplementary to, the law. Officials cited the absence of these regulations when refusing to provide information.

Section 5. Governmental Attitude Regarding International and Nongovernmental Investigation of Alleged Violations of Human Rights

A number of domestic and international human rights groups generally operated without government restrictions, freely investigating and publishing their findings on human rights cases. Although at times government officials were cooperative and responsive to their views, authorities occasionally harassed activists.

Authorities generally agreed to requests for meetings by domestic NGO monitors and followed some NGO recommendations, particularly those related to social welfare, education, and local matters. At the same time, they were usually unresponsive to NGO allegations that law enforcement bodies engaged in mistreatment and abuse. Authorities' usual response in such instances was that they had investigated the allegations but could not corroborate them.

Authorities occasionally harassed human rights groups and civic activists who engaged throughout the year in peaceful protests against a variety of high-profile issues such as an increase in public transportation and tuition costs, illegal construction in residential areas, the presidential decision to join a customs union with Russia, and others. From August 22 through early September, organized groups of six to 12 young men, sometimes armed with clubs and other blunt instruments, attacked activists at different spots in downtown Yerevan, sometimes after following them from protest venues.

On September 5, in one such attack, a group of six or seven men severely beat the project coordinator of media watchdog Yerevan Press Club, Haykak Arshamyan, and a board member of Transparency International, Suren Saghatelyan. The two victims needed hospitalization with multiple abrasions and cuts on their bodies and heads, and Saghatelyan underwent nose surgery. According to the lawyer representing the two victims, police were very slow to act and reluctant to undertake standard forensic procedures.

In addition to the violent attacks, there were multiple reports that police and unknown individuals intimidated and harassed civic activists, including following them and subjecting them to threatening telephone calls.

The protesters and human rights observers alleged the attacks and the harassment occurred with the tacit approval of authorities. As of the end of October, an investigation into these attacks was in progress.

On February 13, a trial court fined resident Tigran Manukyan 30,000 drams ($73) for attacking Arman Veziryan, a member of the Helsinki Association for Human Rights, while he was monitoring pre-election activity of the opposition Armenian

National Congress. Prosecutors initially charged the victim, Veziryan, over the incident but dropped the charges.

Government Human Rights Bodies: The Office of the Human Rights Defender (the ombudsman's office) has a mandate to protect human rights and fundamental freedoms from abuse by the national, regional, and local governments. The effectiveness of the ombudsman was at times limited due to resource constraints. Throughout the year the ombudsman published ad hoc and regular reports on human rights issues. Limited funding made the building housing the ombudsman's office inaccessible for persons in wheelchairs. The government provided no additional funding to the Office of the Ombudsman to carry out its mandate as the National Preventive Mechanism on the Prevention of Torture as provided by the Optional Protocol to the Convention against Torture and Other Cruel, Inhuman, or Degrading Treatment or Punishment.

Section 6. Discrimination, Societal Abuses, and Trafficking in Persons

The constitution and law prohibit discrimination based on race, gender, disability, language, or social status. The government did not effectively enforce these prohibitions.

Women

Rape and Domestic Violence: Rape is a criminal offense and carries a maximum sentence of 15 years; authorities prosecute spousal rape under the general rape statutes. According to official statistics, they registered 14 cases of rape and three of attempted rape during the first nine months of the year, none involving spousal rape. Such crimes continued to be underreported due to social stigma, as well as the absence of female police officers and investigators.

While the law provides penalties for domestic violence that are the same as for other forms of violence, authorities did not effectively prosecute domestic violence. Spousal abuse and violence against women appeared to be widespread. Law-enforcement bodies reported 532 cases of domestic violence during the first nine months of the year, of which 337 involved abuse by a husband, wife, or a partner. Women's rights NGOs reported that, in the period from July 2012 to August 30, domestic violence caused the deaths of eight women and serious injuries to more than a dozen others. Most of the cases occurred in small towns and rural areas.

According to a review of services provided to victims of domestic violence released during the year, there were several ad hoc and permanent shelters in Yerevan and in the regions, all run by NGOs using private or international funding.

According to local observers, most domestic violence continued to go unreported because victims were afraid of physical harm, apprehensive that police would return them to their husbands, or ashamed to disclose their family problems. There were also reports that police were reluctant to act in such cases and discouraged women from filing complaints, especially outside of Yerevan. The majority of domestic violence cases were of low or medium gravity. In such cases a victim can decline to press charges, and perpetrators often pressured victims who reported domestic violence to withdraw charges or recant previous testimony.

According to media experts and women's rights NGOs, locally produced soap operas, popular and frequent on all television channels, appeared to legitimize violence against women and spread intolerance toward homosexuals.

On October 31, member of the Republican Party and president of the Armenian Football Federation, Ruben Hayrapetyan, stated in a press conference that no Armenian man would allow his daughter to play football (soccer), that a man has to lead the family, and Armenian men and women "should not be equal to each other."

In 2012 the NGO Women's Resource Center in Goris published a report on bride kidnapping based on interviews with 150 married women from the southern Syunik region. The report concluded that bride kidnapping was common practice and assumed a variety of forms, ranging from romantic elopement to coercive abduction. One in five respondents was barely acquainted with or did not know their kidnapper. According to the report, 9 percent of respondents were forced to have sex the day/night of their kidnapping. The majority of kidnapped women married their kidnappers. While most of the respondents were in love with the persons they married, others married due to shame, despair, or because their family did not allow them to return home. During the year there were reports of prosecutions of bride kidnapping cases.

On June 24, the Office of the Prosecutor General reopened an investigation that police had suspended into the July 2012 death, originally ascribed to suicide, of Maro Guloyan of the Kotayk region. While authorities initially opened a criminal case against the husband on charges of inducing suicide, Guloyan's family believed that the husband, Gevorg Guloyan, killed his wife, who was pregnant, on the day she decided to leave him. After successfully demanding an exhumation of the body, the family discovered numerous injuries on Maro Guloyan's body not recorded during the autopsy. According to the family's lawyer, the body did not exhibit signs associated with death from suicide by hanging. The lawyer noted many other discrepancies throughout the investigation and alleged that law enforcement bodies protected the husband, a relative of the mayor of Abovyan, the administrative center of the region. As of November 18, the investigation was in progress.

Sexual Harassment: The law does not specifically prohibit sexual harassment, although it addresses lewd acts and indecent behavior. While there was no public data on the extent of the problem, observers believed sexual harassment of women in the workplace was widespread.

In August there were multiple reports of sexual harassment of female activists by police during protest actions, including verbal harassment and groping that took place while police detained the activists. In one case a police officer, later identified as senior sergeant Hakob Khachatryan, was photographed apparently kissing or attempting to kiss an activist on the neck at a protest action on August 24. According to the activist, the officer had been harassing her throughout the day. On August 29, a female member of the National Assembly and member of the ruling Republican Party, Shushan Petrosyan, stated in a press conference that a kiss was better than battery, and the incident looked very "tender." According to press reports, authorities suspended Khachatryan pending investigation of the case.

Reproductive Rights: According to the law, couples and individuals have the right to decide freely and responsibly the number, spacing, and timing of their children and to have the information and means to do so free from discrimination, coercion, and violence. The male spouse and his parents often made such decisions, including decisions on gender-selective and other abortions. There was little access to, or information about, contraception. Skilled attendance during childbirth was more accessible in large towns and other population centers. There were reports that women, especially those in rural or remote areas, faced insufficient access to general and reproductive healthcare services.

Discrimination: Men and women enjoy equal legal status under family law, labor law, property law, inheritance law, and in the judicial system, but discrimination based on gender was a continuing problem in both the public and private sectors. Women generally did not enjoy the same professional opportunities or wages as men, and employers often relegated them to more menial or low-paying jobs.

While providing all parties in a workplace relationship "legal equality," the labor code does not explicitly require equal pay for equal work, and according to official data for 2010, there was a significant gap between the average monthly salary of men and women, and the average monthly salary for younger women was higher than that for older women. Women remained underrepresented in leadership positions in all branches and at all levels of government.

On May 20, the National Assembly adopted a law on Equal Rights of Men and Women and on Ensuring Equal Opportunities. The adoption of the law sparked a debate in the society around the concepts of "gender" and "gender equality." Some groups began disseminating misinformation on social network sites, targeting women's NGOs, and rights defenders. These groups manipulated the wording of the law and began to associate "gender equality" with homosexuality, propaganda, and pedophilia. Women's rights defenders were labeled "traitors of the nation," "destroyers of families," and a "threat to Armenian values." Some materials reportedly called for violence and destruction of property, targeting women's organizations and LGBT persons.

On August 23 and September 3, the Women's Resource Center reported to police bomb threats that it had received through Facebook. Police identified one of the two Facebook users who made the threats but did not initiate a criminal case because the person identified reportedly repented. On November 25, the Women's Council chaired by the prime minister issued a statement expressing concern over the existing tension in the society generated by the misinterpretation of the terms "gender," "gender equality," and "gender identity," as well over the information campaign against women's NGOs. The council urged law enforcement bodies to be more vigilant in order to prevent such cases and, if needed, to punish the perpetrators strictly. The statement also reaffirmed the government's commitment to uphold its obligations under domestic and international law to protect and promote women's rights.

Gender-based Sex Selection: The government continued to support surveys about gender-based sex selection in the country. According to the most recent survey released by the UN Population Fund in May, the ratio of boy-to-girl births in various regions of the country ranged from 111 to 124 boys per 100 girls in case of firstborns, and 160 boys per 100 girls in case of second or next children. The government has not taken measures to address the gender imbalance.

Children

Birth Registration: Children derive citizenship from their parents, and birth registration is a parental responsibility. Observers indicated that some parents, particularly the poorest and most socially disadvantaged, could not register their children at birth, in part because of the cost of transportation to registration centers. Lack of birth registration potentially deprived such children of access to essential social services and increased their vulnerability. During the year international donors continued to work with authorities to address the problem. According to UNICEF data, the births of 96 percent of children born in 2000-10 were registered.

Child Abuse: In 2011 the domestic branch of international NGO Save the Children published an assessment of child abuse in the regions of Kotayk, Aragatsotn, and Shirak. According to the report, family members at times subjected children to physical and psychological abuse and neglect, particularly by failing to provide adequate food, clothing, and shelter. Children reported abuse outside the home as well, including physical and psychological abuse in institutions, schools, and occasionally on the streets.

Forced and Early Marriage: According to April 30 amendments to the family code, the minimum age for marriage is 18 for both boys and girls, although the code permits marriage at age 17 with the consent of parents or guardians and at age 16 given the consent of parents or guardians and if the other intending spouse is at least 18. According to UNICEF for 2000-10 an average of 10 percent of children (boys and girls) married by age 18. Human rights observers expressed concerns over the lowering of the marriage age.

Sexual Exploitation of Children: Antitrafficking statutes prohibit the sexual exploitation of children and provide for sentences of seven to 15 years in prison for trafficking of children, depending on whether aggravating circumstances are present. Child pornography is punishable by imprisonment for up to seven years.

Statutory rape, defined by law as sexual acts with a person under 16 years old, is punishable by a fine and up to two years in prison. According to domestic observers, the legal framework was inadequate for assessing and prosecuting sexual crimes involving children. Sexual solicitation of minors and the failure to report statutory rape are not crimes.

Institutionalized Children: On July 3, the public monitoring group of boarding schools and special educational institutions, composed of NGO representatives, released the findings of its April-July 2012 monitoring of 19 such institutions. According to the report, virtually all the rights of institutionalized children were violated or at risk. Despite the government's proclaimed objective of deinstitutionalizing children, more than 4,000 children remained under institutional care. Eighty percent of institutionalized children had families. According to experts, corruption was the primary reason that deinstitutionalization did not work, since the government based funding for the various state-run orphanages, boarding institutions, and special schools on the number of its residents. One NGO report noted that employees of the monitored institutions confided that, at the beginning of every academic year, each staff member had to enroll two children in the boarding institution to maintain his or her job. According to the report, children in the monitored institutions were also not fully protected from violence, neglect, and humiliating punishment. In many cases institution staff did not view the methods used as violence, describing their actions as punishment for bad behavior. Children talking about the violence also viewed it as a necessary measure for bad behavior and disobedience. According to the report, 16 of the monitored institutions used methods that demonstrated a clear record of physical and psychological violence toward children.

After reviewing the situation in the country, the UN Committee on the Rights of the Child issued a report on June 14, which urged authorities to investigate individual cases of violence in closed or partially closed institutions and to prosecute and punish perpetrators. It recommended that authorities prohibit the use of corporal punishment in all settings and provide for legislatively based enforcement mechanisms, including appropriate sanctions in cases of violation.

International Child Abductions: The country is a party to the 1980 Hague Convention on the Civil Aspects of International Child Abduction.

Anti-Semitism

Observers estimated the size of the country's Jewish population at between 500 and 1,000 persons. There were no reports of anti-Semitic acts.

Trafficking in Persons

See the Department of State's *Trafficking in Persons Report* at www.state.gov/j/tip/.

Persons with Disabilities

While the law prohibits discrimination against persons with any disability, in employment, education, access to health care, and the provision of other state services, discrimination remained a problem. The law and a special government decree mandate accessibility to buildings, including schools, for persons with disabilities, but very few buildings or other facilities were accessible. The Ministry of Labor and Social Affairs is responsible for protecting the rights of persons with disabilities but failed to do so effectively.

Persons with disabilities seldom went outside their homes due to the social stigma associated with disabilities. At times children with disabilities missed school, due both to discrimination and the absence of facilities to accommodate their needs. According to a survey conducted during 2012 by UNICEF, one in five children with disabilities did not attend school, and one in eight resided in a residential care institution (orphanage or special boarding school). Only one in 20 of those children had access to mainstream education, while five in 20 went to special schools and 14 in 20 did not go to school at all. According to official data for 2012, 64.8 percent of children with disabilities were poor, and an additional 8.4 percent were extremely poor.

Persons with all types of disabilities experienced problems in virtually all spheres of life, including health care, social and psychological rehabilitation, education, transportation, communication, access to employment, and social protection. Social acceptance was even more difficult for women with disabilities. Access to information and communications was a particularly significant problem for persons with sensory disabilities. Penitentiaries lacked adequate accommodations for persons with disabilities.

Hospitals, residential care, and other facilities for persons with serious disabilities remained substandard. According to official data, more than 90 percent of persons with disabilities who were able to work were unemployed.

Societal Abuses, Discrimination, and Acts of Violence Based on Sexual Orientation and Gender Identity

No antidiscrimination laws apply to sexual orientation or gender identity. Societal attitudes toward LGBT persons remained highly negative, with society generally viewing homosexuality as a medical affliction. Societal discrimination based on sexual orientation and gender identity negatively affected employment, family relations, and access to education and health care.

During the year a proposed law against discrimination prepared by the ombudsman's office, which initially included a provision on LBGT persons, sparked a wave of homophobia. This proposed law, paired with developments related to the adoption of the law on Equal Rights of Men and Women and on Ensuring Equal Opportunities, further marginalized LGBT persons and the few NGOs working to advance the human rights of LGBT persons, since the latter preferred to keep a low profile to avoid possible attacks against them, both verbal and physical (see section 6, Women).

In August the NGO New Generation presented the results of a survey of attitudes toward LGBT persons among human rights organizations in the regions of the country. The survey revealed a low level of awareness and mostly negative attitudes toward LGBT persons, with some respondents expressing the view that homosexuality was a disease and the best way to help LGBT persons was to "cure" them.

On July 25, a trial court convicted brothers Arameh and Hambik Mkritch Khapazyan and gave them two-year suspended sentences for the May 2012 firebombing of the DIY Bar in Yerevan, a popular spot for activists who promoted equal rights for women and minorities, including LGBT persons. The court also fined the brothers 3,227,563 drams ($7,900) for damages incurred by the bar owner. The brothers had admitted their guilt and the trial proceeded using an expedited procedure, a judicial provision somewhat similar to plea-bargaining.

Openly gay men were exempt from military service, purportedly because of concern fellow service members would abuse them. An exemption required a medical finding, based on a psychological examination, that an individual had a mental disorder; this information appeared in the individual's personal documents.

According to human rights activists, sexual minorities were frequent targets for humiliating discrimination in prisons, where authorities forced them to perform degrading labor and separated them from the rest of the prison population.

Other Societal Violence or Discrimination

There were no reports during the year of acts of societal violence or discrimination against persons with HIV/AIDS. The UN Committee on the Rights of the Child in its June 14 concluding observations noted its concern over the de facto discrimination against certain categories of children, including those living with HIV.

Many employers reportedly discriminated against potential employees by age, most commonly requiring job applicants to be between the ages of 18 and 30. For example, during the year the city of Yerevan posted a job vacancy for tour operators, specifying that they be below 30 years of age. While this discrimination appeared to be widespread, authorities did not take any action to mitigate it. After age 40, unemployed workers, particularly women, had little chance of finding jobs appropriate to their education or skills.

Section 7. Worker Rights

a. Freedom of Association and the Right to Collective Bargaining

The law protects the right of workers, except for personnel of the armed forces and law enforcement agencies, to form and to join independent unions. The law also provides for the right to strike, with the same exceptions, and permits collective bargaining. The law stipulates that workers' rights cannot be restricted because of membership in a union. A list of justifiable grounds for firing a worker, enumerated in the labor code, does not include union activity.

The government did not always respect labor rights. Labor organizations remained weak because of employer resistance, high unemployment, and poor economic conditions. Labor unions were generally inactive with the exception of those connected with the mining and chemical industries. There were small-scale protests by workers due to dissatisfaction with delayed salary payments and against violation of labor contracts and dangerous working conditions. Unions were tied closely to the government. There were no reports during the year of specific acts of antiunion discrimination, but there were reports in past years that some mining enterprises, including some financed by foreign investors, discouraged employees from joining labor unions and defending their rights in court with the implied threat of loss of employment.

b. Prohibition of Forced or Compulsory Labor

The law prohibits all forms of forced and compulsory labor, and the government effectively enforced such laws. Through September the government investigated three, and prosecuted two, cases of labor trafficking, the only reported instances of forced labor.

Also see the Department of State's *Trafficking in Persons Report* at www.state.gov/j/tip/.

c. Prohibition of Child Labor and Minimum Age for Employment

There are laws and policies to protect children from exploitation in the workplace. The minimum age for employment is 16, but children may work from the age of 14 with permission of a parent or a guardian. The law prohibits persons under 18 from working overtime; in harmful, strenuous, or dangerous conditions; at night; or on holidays.

There were few reports of child labor. According to the 2010 Armenia Demographic and Health Survey, 4 percent of children were involved in child labor, most of them in family businesses.

On June 14, the UN Committee on the Rights of the Child issued a report noting its concern over significant numbers of children, including those below the age of 14, who were dropping out of schools to work in informal sectors such as agriculture, car service, construction and gathering of waste metal, and family businesses. The committee expressed particular concern about the increasing number of children involved in begging in the streets and in heavy manual labor, such as laborers and loaders. It also expressed concern that labor inspectorates were not effective in controlling child labor.

Also see the Department of Labor's *Findings on the Worst Forms of Child Labor* at www.dol.gov/ilab/programs/ocft/tda.htm.

d. Acceptable Conditions of Work

The monthly minimum wage was 45,000 drams ($110). According to the most recent official estimate from 2011, the extreme poverty line was 21,306 drams ($52) and the general poverty line was 29,856 drams ($73).

The law provides for a 40-hour workweek, 20 days of mandatory annual leave, and compensation for overtime and nighttime work. The law provides that compulsory overtime cannot exceed four hours in two consecutive days and 180 hours within a year. Authorities did not effectively enforce these standards. Many private sector employees, particularly in the service sector, were unable to obtain paid leave and were required to work more than eight hours a day without additional compensation. According to representatives of some employment agencies, many employers also continued to hire employees for a "probationary" period of 10 to 30 days, during which they were not paid. Often employers subsequently dismissed these employees and they were unable to claim payment for the time they worked because their initial employment was undocumented.

Government decree established occupational and health standards. The State Labor Inspectorate, with 126 inspectors, was responsible for enforcing these standards but did not do so effectively. During the year the State Labor Inspectorate reportedly made little progress toward implementing an inspection regime or enforcing the labor code, and its work was reportedly undermined by corruption. In August through a government decree, the State Labor Inspectorate was moved from the Ministry of Labor and Social Affairs and merged with the Ministry of Healthcare. Observers noted that the State Labor Inspectorate did not have sufficient resources or staff. Inspectors primarily concentrated on social security payments and other tax-related issues instead of safety standards and protection of workers' rights. Managers of enterprises that were the primary employers in certain poor areas frequently took advantage of the absence of alternative jobs and neglected issues related to adequate pay, job safety, and environmental concerns. Workers in the informal sector did not benefit from any form of governmental protection.

Work safety and health conditions remained substandard in numerous sectors, and there were several fatal workplace incidents during the year.